In My Backyard

I SEE A WORM

By Agatha Gregson

Gareth Stevens
PUBLISHING

Please visit our website, www.garethstevens.com. For a free color catalog of all our high-quality books, call toll free 1-800-542-2595 or fax 1-877-542-2596.

Library of Congress Cataloging-in-Publication Data

Names: Gregson, Agatha, author.
Title: I see a worm / Agatha Gregson.
Description: New York : Gareth Stevens Publishing, [2019] | Series: In my backyard | Includes index.
Identifiers: LCCN 2018013468| ISBN 9781538228760 (library bound) | ISBN 9781538231845 (paperback) | ISBN 9781538231852 (6 pack)
Subjects: LCSH: Worms–Juvenile literature.
Classification: LCC QL386.6 .G75 2019 | DDC 592/.3–dc23
LC record available at https://lccn.loc.gov/2018013468

First Edition

Published in 2019 by
Gareth Stevens Publishing
111 East 14th Street, Suite 349
New York, NY 10003

Editor: Therese Shea
Designer: Sarah Liddell

Photo credits: Cover, p. 1 viktor_kov/Shutterstock.com; p. 5 Anastasia Kozhevnikova/Shutterstock.com; p. 7 BERNATSKII IURII/Shutterstock.com; p. 9 PHOTO FUN/Shutterstock.com; p. 11 Carlos Banyuls/ Shutterstock.com; pp. 13, 24 (setae) J-rg Lcking/EyeEm/EyeEm/Getty Images; p. 15 Witaya Proadtayakogool/ Shutterstock.com; p. 17 Fir0002/Wikimedia Commons; pp. 19, 24 (garden) Irina Fischer/Shutterstock.com; p. 21 Jukka Palm/Shutterstock.com; p. 23 Petr Bonek/Shutterstock.com.

Printed in the United States of America

CPSIA compliance information: Batch #CW19GS: For further information contact Gareth Stevens, New York, New York at 1-800-542-2595.

Contents

I see a worm.
It's an earthworm!

Earthworms have
soft bodies.
Some are very long!

Earthworms have
no bones.

They have no legs
or eyes!

Earthworm bodies
have hairs.
The hairs are called setae.

Setae help them move.
They help them dig.

Earthworms live in dirt.
They eat dirt!

They are good
for gardens.
They make dirt healthy!

Many animals eat worms.
Birds eat worms!

I like to watch earthworms!

Words to Know

garden

setae

Index